# Embracing Excellence

# Embracing Excellence

## A 31-Day Journey Through Proverbs 31

### Carolyn Tatem

FOREVER
*publishing*

FOREVER PUBLISHING, LLC

Embracing Excellence, A 31-Day Journey through Proverbs 31

Copyright ©2015 by Carolyn Tatem

Forever Publishing, LLC
PO Box 1061
Brandywine, MD 20613

Library of Congress Control Number: 2015917873

ISBN: 978-0-9962851-4-8

*Cover design by* AugustPride, LLC
*Interior design and layout by* Rick Soldin

Printed in the United States of America

To all of the ladies who desire to be a woman of excellence and all of the men who want to find a woman with excellent qualities.

# Contents

# Introduction

This book is dedicated to those who want to embrace God's excellent plan for their lives. It is my prayer that women will read it and be inspired to allow God to shape, make and mold them into a woman of excellence. Young men can also benefit by reading this book. *Embracing Excellence* defines the type of woman that every good man would love to have. I pray that men will use this book to get an idea of the type of woman God wants them to have. Prayerfully, the things that are high on God's list will also be high on your list. A good woman is hard to find especially if you don't know what you're looking for.

For years, I have been saying that my favorite woman in the Bible is the *Proverbs 31* Woman. It wasn't until I began studying this woman that I learned that this was not a physical woman. This is a woman of excellence who represents the goal that all women should be moving towards. Don't worry; you can't accomplish this goal alone; it is only as you move closer to God that He develops and transforms you to be a woman of excellence. We can learn so much through studying the *Proverbs 31* Woman. She inspires us to be all that we can be.

# *Wise Teachings*

*When you get wisdom, share it with others.*

**Proverbs 31:1 (NKJV)**

*"The words of King Lemuel, the utterance which his mother taught him."*

*A*t the age of twelve, I remember giving my life to the Lord. My grandmother took me to church right around Easter. She had not been to church for a while and went to restore her relationship with God. After the sermon was preached, my grandmother decided to rededicate herself to God and walked down to the altar; I went behind her. At the time, I didn't fully understand all that was happening. However, I remember going into a prayer room and accepting Christ as my Lord and Savior. From that point on, going to church became a weekly event for my grandmother and me. I loved being in God's house.

My grandmother and I went to Friday night Bible study, church activities on Saturday, Sunday school before church on Sunday mornings and evening service. Each time that I attended church, I would hear wise teachings. The pastor would teach from the Word of God and explain in such a way that a child could understand. He would teach young and old how to live for God. The more that I attended, the more that I received wisdom and learned how God wanted me to live. Not only did God use the pastor, He also used many of the people that he placed in my life to speak words of wisdom. The following are some of the wise teachings that I received.

I was taught that God should be my number one priority, so having a relationship with God became very important to me. As a result, I maintained a close walk with God from adolescence to adulthood. I was also taught the value of my body and how God didn't want me to share my body with anyone until marriage. I can remember the pastor teaching about how the body is precious and that a man is not worthy of your body unless he is your husband. This really stuck with me.

My mom taught me to be a good student, strive for excellence and make good grades. There were a few young adults at church who had been to college and encouraged me to go. They even helped me to apply for college and shared with me the value of higher education. This was such an important part of my journey because I was the first one in my family to go to college and graduate. I am so thankful to God for everyone that God used to provide wise teachings that have helped to shape my life and to make me strive for excellence.

## *Embracing Excellence*

In *Proverbs 31:1,* King Lemuel is beginning to share wise teachings that he received from his mother. King Lemuel's name means "devoted to God" and his mom taught him how to live up to his name. If we are going to be devoted to God, we must embrace His principles and strive for excellence.

To embrace is "to receive gladly, eagerly, or to willingly accept." To be excellent is "to possess an outstanding quality." Are you willing to embrace God's will and His ways for your life? Will you allow God to develop excellence in you? The Bible is God's holy book filled with wise teachings. This is why it is so important to read God's Word. As we read, He fills us with His wisdom and teaches us how to live. Wise teaching can also come from your parents, grandparents, pastor, and the authorities in your life or anyone who God chooses to use.

# *Journal*

1. **What does embracing excellence mean to you?**

   *Finding the things I can excell at and sticking to it!*

2. **When you were younger, what was a wise teaching that you embraced?**

   *To respect and love yourself!*

3. **What wise teaching can you share to help someone else?**

   *That you will never truely love yourself until you realize the love God has for you as his beloved child*

4. **Have you ever ignored a wise teaching? How did it affect your life?**

   *Yes, I made mistakes.*
   *I was told to not have sex till marriage and since I did to early it is difficult to manage a relationship about marriage until then have already went to far. How do we go back?*

# Prayer

*God, help me to embrace the wise teachers and teachings that You have placed in my life. Forgive me for the times that I have not obeyed. Teach me to recognize when You are speaking or using others to speak to me. Help me to happily receive Your Word, Your will and Your ways from whatever source You may use.* **Amen.**

# Set High Standards

*If you don't stand for something, you will fall for anything!*

**Proverbs 31:2 (NKJV)**

*"What, my son?
And what, son of my womb?
And what, son of my vows?"*

When I first became a Christian, I joined a church and was under the leadership of the late Bishop Lewis T. Tait, Sr. One of the many sayings of Bishop Lewis T. Tait, Sr. was that; "If you don't stand for something, you will fall for anything!" It is because of his wise teachings that I developed a high standard for my body at the age of twelve. I was taught that my body was precious and that you only get one body. Bishop Tait encouraged the young people to wait until they were married to have sex. He set the standards so high and had sayings that he would repeat over and over throughout his sermons. It's been over 30 years now, but I can still hear him saying: 1) Keep your dress down and your drawers up! 2) Why should a man buy the cow if he can get the milk for free? 3) Anything worth having is worth waiting for! Each of these sayings helped me to set a high standard for my life and for my body. I decided that no one would have my body until I was married. I believed that my body is precious and that no man would have it until he was my husband. At the age of twelve, I decreed and declared that I would wait until I was married to have sex. I set a high standard for myself based on the "what" that I was taught at the early age of 12.

## Embracing Excellence

In *Proverbs 31:2,* the "what" signifies a high standard that King Lemuel's mother shared with her son. The "what" represents: What you will do, what you ought to do and what not to do. King Lemuel's mom prepared her son by sharing her thoughts, advice and high standards for him. When she said; "What my son? And what son of my womb? And what, son of my vows?" As a mother myself, I picture her personalizing the fact that this is my son, I gave birth to you, you came out of my womb, and you are the child that God gave me whom I have vowed to take care of. I vowed to teach you right and raise you by God's standards so listen as I teach you what you need to know. Mothers have the ability to fashion their children's minds and thoughts. King Lemuel's mother shared her standards for her son.

Imagine God saying these exact words to you: "What, my daughter? And what, daughter of my womb? And what, daughter of my vows?" God has the "what" for each one of us. He has given us His instructions. He has set high standards for each of us. He wants us to live by His instructions, the Word of God. Are you willing to take time to learn the "what" that God had in mind when He created you? Please know that every day that you have breath in your body, God is giving you an opportunity to live out the "what" which are the standards that He has for you.

## *Journal*

1. What standards have you set for your life?

2. What is it that God wants you to do, but you have not done?

3.  Are you willing to live by God's standards?

4.  How can regular time in prayer and Bible reading help you to know the "what" for your life?

# Prayer

*Lord, please help me to know the standards that You have for my life. Forgive me for where I have fallen short from the standards that You have for me. Teach me the "what" that You have for me. Help me to obey.* **Amen.**

# Don't Give Up Your Strength

*Be strong and resist those things that make you weak.*

**Proverbs 31:3 (NKJV)**

*"Do not give your strength to women,
Nor your ways to that which destroys kings."*

*O*ne of the things that I can remember my mother saying when I was a teenager is to not get so tied up with a boy that I get off track. My grandmother would say that you could tell when a girl had been with a boy sexually because her behavior would change. Therefore, I was encouraged to focus on my school work, make good grades and worry about a boyfriend later. So, I never really had a serious boyfriend while I was a teenager. I did have a few male friends here and there but most of our time was spent on the phone talking. Even as I got older, I spent very little time dating. One of the things that I noticed about my friends who were dating and spending time with a young man was that they changed. They became very attached to the guy. I never understood the deep attachment, but now I do. In many of those cases, they were sleeping with the guy and experiencing a level of attachment that I had not. What I later observed is that sex really did change things; my grandmother was right. In other words, sex outside of marriage really zaps you. Since sex was created by God to bond a husband and wife together, when a person participates before marriage, it gives a person a part of you that God never intended for them to have. This is why it is so important to wait "until it pleases" (Song of *Solomon 8:4*). Wait until you are married to combine your body with someone else's body. It will take your strength.

It took me years to realize that it was the sex that was changing my friends. They were bonding with girls and guys behind closed doors and not realizing the effect that it was having on them. The young ladies in our church were taught that sex ties and bonds people together and the only man that God wants us to sexually bond with is our husband. The only woman that God wants a man to sexually bond with is his wife. Not everyone listened but for some reason this kept me holding on until marriage. Once a couple has pre-marital sex, it bonds them together and it complicates the relationship. This makes breaking up very difficult. Sleeping with multiple partners bonds you with multiple people and can only create even more problems emotionally and physically. These problems can take your strength and make the body weak. Don't give up your strength!

## *Embracing Excellence*

In *Proverbs 31:3,* King Lemuel's mother says "Do not give your strength to women, nor your ways to that which destroys kings." Notice that this mother is telling her son not to give his strength to women. Strength is defined as "the quality of being strong, mental power and power by reason of influence." Studies reveal that the strength of the body is weakened by excessive sex. Lemuel's mom didn't want her son to get caught up in having sex with woman after woman. She knew that this would zap his strength and she warned him by saying, "Do not give your strength to women."

In the ancient world, kings were known to sleep with many women. This behavior destroyed many rulers. Today leaders are still being destroyed for this behavior. Not only does sex affect your body, but your mind and your spirit. King Lemuel's mom was making it clear to her son that she did not want him to be weakened by his pursuit of women or anything else. She knew that if her son gave his body or his mind over to women, it would affect his thinking and his behavior. Sex with a multiplicity of partners impairs your body, strength of mind and your ability to reason. Apparently, this mom had seen the impact of excessive sex with other kings and she didn't want her son to go down the same path; this is why she warns him. We can learn from this warning and share the same information with our sons and our daughters.

## *Journal*

1. What lessons can you learn from the instructions of King Lemuel's mother?

2. How does pre-marital sex or sex with multiple people affect a person?

3. What is God saying to you about *Proverbs 31:3?*

4. Have you ever been so tied up into a woman or man that it consumed you?

## Prayer

*Lord, thank You for the warning in Proverbs 31:3. Help me to take heed to the warning and share it with others. Even though we live in a world that is sexually active, help me to be obedient to You. Please forgive me for giving my strength to the wrong persons or the wrong things. Help me to treasure my body and to only do what pleases You.* **Amen.**

# It's Not for You

*Some things are just not for you!*

**Proverbs 31:4 (NKJV)**

"It is not for kings, O Lemuel,
It is not for kings to drink wine,
Nor for princes intoxicating drink;"

*H*ave you ever been some place or tried something that you knew was not for you? Maybe you did it because someone talked you in to it, everybody else was doing it or because someone you knew introduced you to it. After you did it, you realized that it wasn't for you.

Some things are just not good for the body. Wine, alcohol, illicit drugs or any other substance that will alter the way that you think or feel can cause a problem. When people are drunk or intoxicated, they tend to do and say some foolish things. They may even hurt people while they are under the influence. The abuse of alcohol can cause a relationship or family to be destroyed. When a woman or man decides to make drinking alcohol a regular part of their life and a regular way to cope with life, it creates problems. Many families have suffered because daddy or mommy was out getting drunk. Once a family member allows alcohol to take control, they are usually no good to the family. Alcohol impairs a person's behavior and thinking. Sometimes life can be so challenging that people go to alcohol to soothe their pains and calm their fears. However, only God has the power to soothe our pains and calm our fears.

## Embracing Excellence

In *Proverbs 31:4*, King Lemuel's mom says, "It is not for kings, O Lemuel, It is not for Kings to drink wine, nor for princes intoxicating drink." King Lemuel's mother was giving him words of wisdom. She made it clear that drinking wine or any intoxicating drink was not for him. As a king, she did not want him to be put in a position to make a fool out of himself. She wanted him to be a wise king. When a person is drinking wine or any intoxicating drink, they tend to lose control over their actions and their speech.

God has the same message for us. He doesn't want us drinking wine or any intoxicating drink. These things have a way of altering our thinking, judgment or our actions. God doesn't want us to be led by alcohol or an intoxicating drink. He wants us to be led by Him and His Holy Spirit. Be very careful about what you put into your body. When a person accepts Jesus Christ as their Lord and Savior, the body is the temple of the Holy Spirit. *Proverbs 31:4* instructs us to be different and realize that everything, "Is not for you!"

Drinking wine and intoxicating drinks invite a different kind of spirit to come over you and it's not holy. It is interesting that outside of many of the liquor stores there is a sign that says, "Wine and Spirits." Many Christians justify drinking wine because wine is mentioned in the Bible. Yes it is mentioned, but God makes it clear that drinking wine or any intoxicating drink is not a practice for those who desire to live godly. *Proverbs 20:1* says, "Wine is a mocker, strong drink is raging and whosoever is deceived thereby is not wise."

# *Journal*

1.  Have you ever had an intoxicating drink or seen someone drunk before?

2. How did the drink make you feel or how did it alter the person's behavior?

3. Why do you think King Lemuel's mother advised him against drinking wine and alcohol?

4. Whose influence would you rather be under, an intoxicating drink or the Holy Spirit?

# Prayer

*Lord, I thank You for this body that You have given to me. Please keep me from putting anything in my body that would alter the way that I think, act or treat others. Help me to be filled with Your Holy Spirit and not with wine and other spirits.* **Amen.**

# Don't Be Led Astray

*Choose actions that draw you closer to God, not away from God.*

**Proverbs 31:5 (NKJV)**

*"Lest they drink and forget the law,
And pervert the justice of all the afflicted."*

*W*hat's the first thing that you normally do when you get up? Do you watch television, check Facebook, read your email or the newspaper? How do you normally spend the first few minutes of your day? What is your goal for each day? Every day we have a choice. We can choose activities that line up and lead us closer to God and God's Word or we can choose activities that lead us astray. Which will you choose?

When we want to draw closer to God we must pick activities that involve Him. Our minds should be fixed on how we can bring glory and honor to God in the way that we walk and the way that we talk. This means starting and ending our days with God in mind. How can this be done? *Matthew 6:33* tells us to "Seek ye first the kingdom of God and His righteousness and all these things will be added unto you." When we first wake up in the morning, we ought to give God some praise and spend time with Him. God wants us to enjoy His presence and His promises. This means that He wants us to take pleasure in praying and spending time in the Word to hear what He has to say on a regular basis. He loves you and wants us to love Him. We can demonstrate our love for Him through our obedience to Him and His Word.

There are so many things that God wants to tell us and reveal to us but we must be willing to spend time with Him. Spending time with God sets the tone for each day. As we spend time with Him, He leads us and guides us to make righteous choices and to have righteous behavior.

# Embracing Excellence

In *Proverbs 31:5,* King Lemuel's mother says, "Lest they drink and forget the law, and pervert the justice of all the afflicted." She did not want her son to drink wine or any intoxicating drink because doing so would cause him to forget the law. For years, alcohol has been known to cloud the minds and lead to injustice and poor decisions. There have been many cases where leaders, athletes, parents, etc., have been under the influence of alcohol and made bad decisions. Some have lost their lives, their family and their careers all in the name of alcohol. Forgetting the law and making bad choices are often the result of drinking an intoxicating drink.

So what habit or behavior do you have that can cause you to forget God's law? Each one of us has some behavior or activity that if left unchecked, can cause us to forget God's law. It could be something so simple like spending hours on the computer but spending no time with God. God wants us to draw closer to Him (*James 4:8*). He says when you come closer to Him, He will come closer to you. The main point for this chapter is that we must let go of any activity or behavior that leads us astray. We must decrease our time in those activities that may not be bad but when given too much time they cause us to forget God's laws. When we forget God's law or when we are led astray, it affects other people. Our spouse, children, family, co-workers and anyone who is connected to us can be negatively affected when we forget God's law. How you live your life can either help lead others to Christ or lead them astray. King Lemuel's mom wanted her son to remember God's Word so that He could think righteous thoughts, have righteous behavior and make righteous decisions.

# *Journal*

1. What is the first thing that you normally do within the first few minutes of your day?

2. What activities draw you closer to God's law and what takes you away?

3. Do you have friends or family in your life who cause you to go astray?

4. What do you need to change in order to spend more time with God?

# Prayer

*Thank You Lord for Your love and kindness towards me. Help me to demonstrate more love towards You through my actions and my obedience. Increase my desire to spend more time with You and in Your Word. Teach me Your will and Your ways so that I can exemplify You in all of my actions. Help me to draw closer to You so that I can be a better me and lead others towards You. Help me not to allow anything to lead me astray.* **Amen.**

# The World's Way or God's Way

*Choose for yourselves this day whom you will serve.*
—Joshua 24:15 (NJKV)

**Proverbs 31:6 (NKJV)**

*"Give strong drink to him who is perishing,
And wine to those who are bitter of heart."*

*H*ow do you handle the challenges of life? Life can present some challenges and difficulties that make it hard to move on. Each of us must decide how we will cope when our plans don't go the way we would like, when challenges and unexpected things happen in our relationships, finances, family, etc. Some people trust God to see them through and some turn to other people and things to help them cope.

Wine and alcohol are strong drinks that are known to bring excitement to the spirit. Many turn to wine and alcohol to help them get through the difficulties in life. History reveals that there are many uses for the strong drink. For years, people have been drinking to ease their pain and forget their troubles. There was a time in the Jewish culture where a cup of wine was given to mourners and criminals on their way to execution to help them deal with their pain and suffering. One of the purposes of the strong drink is to help control a man's mind and body. It was used as a restorative and remedial tool to help change a man from being bitter or bad. In some cases, wine was medicated and used as a medicine; this is when it was properly administered. Today, people are still running to wine and alcohol to help them deal with life and the challenges of this world. However, these things can only provide a temporary solution.

God offers permanent solutions and He wants to be the One who we turn to when we are dealing with the challenges of life. When we feel discouraged or discomforted, the Holy Spirit wants to be our Comforter. He said that He would never leave us nor forsake us. He wants us to cast every one of our cares on Him because He cares for us (*I Peter 5:7*). When we take our cares to the Lord, He promises to sustain us. If we are dealing with heaviness or sadness, we must learn to turn to God. When we invite God into the challenges of life, He will give us joy in the midst. The Bible says that He will give us beauty for ashes, the oil of joy for mourning and the garment of praise for the spirit of heaviness (*Isaiah 61:3*).

## Embracing Excellence

*Proverbs 31:6* says, "Give strong drink to him who is perishing. And wine to those who are bitter of heart." Perhaps this verse explains how some kings may have handled the challenges of life. However, King Lemuel's mother was challenging her son to do things differently. She didn't want him to think or act upon the world's way; she wanted him to stick with God's way. We have the same choice. We can accept the world's way of dealing with life or God's way.

As Christians, we must not accept the ways of the world. We must live by the Word of God. The world says get pregnant then get married but God says differently. The world says live with your significant other then get married. In other words "shack up" but God says get married first. The world says that it is alright to be married to the same sex, but God says that marriage is between one man and one woman. The world says that when you are sad or troubled, have a glass of wine to calm you and soothe you. God says that He sent us His Holy Spirit to comfort us. He is our helper, counselor, intercessor, strengthener and our advocate. So each of us has to decide how we will deal with the difficulties and challenges of life. Will we turn to God or to wine and strong drink?

# *Journal*

1. How do you deal with the challenges and difficulties of life?

2. What is the difference between comfort that the world may offer and that God offers?

3. Have you accepted any of the lies that the world has presented?

4. Which direction do you want to take, God's way or the world's way?

# Prayer

*Lord, I thank You for being a very present help in the time of trouble. Please help me to choose Your way and not the way of the world when I am facing challenges and difficulties. Help me to know that You are my peace and that I don't need to turn to a drink to ease my pain. Allow me to embrace Your Holy Spirit and experience the comfort, strength and calmness that He brings. Bless me with joy and gladness when I am feeling sad and low.* **Amen.**

# The Sea of Forgetfulness

*There are some things that you don't want to remember.*

**Proverbs 31:7 (NKJV)**

*"Let him drink and forget his poverty,
And remember his misery no more."*

*H*ave you ever had something happen to you or one of your family members that caused you so much pain that you would like to erase it from your mind? Perhaps it was rape, abuse, divorce, abandonment, rejection, a tragic death or something so evil that you don't even want to talk about it. Every time that you think about what happened it brings tears to your eyes and pain to your heart. These are the type of things that you just want to take out of your mind, erase and throw them into the sea of forgetfulness.

Many years ago, when alcoholic drinks were first discovered, man began using it as a medicine. Believe it or not, alcohol used to be considered as a beneficial and valuable drug. It was given to people for a variety of medicinal purposes. Therefore, when people were sick or sad, they would drink to help heal their bodies and to bring cheerfulness. People would also drink to help them forget about their pain and problems. What's interesting is that today alcohol is known as a depressant. Some people drink when they are happy; however, many still drink to help them cope with their problems and try to erase pain and sorrow.

I have a cousin who was an only child and lost his mother as a young adult. His mother was a single parent and did the best that she could in raising him. She loved the Lord and raised him in the church. Since his mother was the only parent that he knew, his life wasn't the same without her. Losing his mother was very painful and although it has been many years since her death, he is still in pain. In addition to him hurting over his mother's death, my cousin has expressed to me that he is also hurting because he felt mistreated by family members during the time of his mother's funeral. Every now and then, I get a call from him when it sounds as if he has been drinking. Sometimes when people are drunk, they say things that are on their heart and they don't bite their tongue. It seems as if my cousin starts drinking when he remembers the pain of losing his mother and how he was mistreated many years ago. Alcohol is used to help ease the pain. He calls me to discuss things that hurt him and to share the pain that he feels from something that happened many years ago. Some things are so painful that you don't want to remember them.

## Embracing Excellence

*Proverbs 31:7* says, "Let him drink and forget his poverty, and remember his misery no more." No matter what may have happened to you, no matter who hurt you, God knows all about it. He cares for you and He loves you. You can cast every one of your hurts, pains and disappointments on the Lord. He wants to heal your broken heart and restore your life. God wants to be your sustainer (*Psalm 55:22*). Drinking alcohol may temporarily relieve the pain but God offers permanent healing. There is nothing too hard for Him. He will allow the misery that you experienced to become a ministry for others. The very thing that has caused you pain can be used to help someone else. So don't drink your problems and pain away; give them to God.

Giving your problems to God means praying and releasing your hurt to Him on a regular basis. I have found that praying and reading God's word is the best medicine that anyone could ever take. It heals your mind and helps with your thought process. It's our minds and the way that we think that causes us to remember the pain. However, if we learn to replace our way of thinking with God's way of thinking, we can think good thoughts and be healed. *Romans 12:2* says that we are "transformed by the renewing of our minds."

# *Journal*

1. Have you experienced something that causes you so much pain that you want to forget that it ever happened?

2. How do you cope with painful thoughts or painful situations?

3. Do you think that God is pleased with the way that you handle your pain? Why or why not?

4. What does God do when we go to Him with our sins and shortcomings?

# Prayer

*Father, in the name of Jesus, please help me to give You all of my pain and past hurts. I cast every care on You, because I know that You care for me. Help me to never carry the pain again. Heal me, restore me and cause me to think good thoughts. Please forgive me for the times that I have not handled my pain properly.* **Amen.**

*Day 8*

# Speak Up!

*Allow God to use your voice to speak for those who will not speak for themselves.*

**Proverbs 31:8 (NKJV)**

*"Open your mouth for the speechless,
In the cause of all who are appointed to die."*

*H*ave you ever had something that you wanted to say but you were afraid and God used someone around you to say the very thing that you wanted to say? Maybe it was a big brother, big sister, your spouse, a parent or a friend. Many times, my husband is the person who will speak up. My husband and I met while serving in the Youth Ministry at the First Baptist Church of Glenarden. We both volunteered to be youth advisors. Every week we would see each other serving and sometimes we both had to attend meetings with other volunteers and the leaders within the Youth Ministry. One of the things that my husband was known for in any of the meetings was speaking up! He would always say the very thing that others wanted to say, but they were afraid or hesitant. Since we have been married, my husband has consistently been the one who will speak up. Many times I have gone to him to get encouragement to speak up or when appropriate, I have asked him to speak on my behalf. It is as if God has put a boldness in him to say what often needs to be said when others are afraid to say it.

Sometimes I find myself in situations where I am not bold enough to say what needs to be said. I can remember a time where I was in the ladies' room at church and heard a couple of teenage girls talking about marriage. One was discouraging the other from the idea of marriage since, in her observation, everyone gets a divorce. She was encouraging her girlfriend to just have a man and live with him. I overheard this conversation and felt like I should have said something, but I did not. I was afraid to say something because they weren't talking to me. However, I honestly believe that God wanted me to speak on behalf of his institution of marriage. I am sorry to say that I missed that opportunity to speak up. Perhaps God wanted me to provide a different perspective, but I kept silent. I asked God to please forgive me.

## Embracing Excellence

In *Proverbs 31:8,* King Lemuel's mom said, "Open your mouth for the speechless, in the cause of all who are appointed to die." She advised her son to speak up. She wanted him to open his mouth and speak freely for those who could not speak for themselves. If he did not speak up for some of the people, they would be put to death. In the ancient world, kings were responsible for defending the weak and helping the helpless. It was important for a king to emulate the King of Kings who is a Defender of all who are weak and helpless.

God wants to use us to speak up! There may be someone in our surroundings who is timid, bashful, or fearful that you may have to speak for. Maybe you are the one who is timid, bashful, or fearful and God wants you to speak up! Some people are headed for destruction unless someone speaks on their behalf. King Lemuel's mom wanted him to have wisdom, power and to use his authority to speak up for those who could not speak for themselves. God has an assignment for you and you have to be willing to open your mouth and speak on God's behalf. Often, God works through people. We are His mouth piece, but we must be willing to be used and to say what He wants us to say. Will you speak up? Will you allow God to use you to speak on behalf of others? Perhaps God wants to use your voice to save someone from death and destruction. Will you speak?

# *Journal*

1.  Have you been in a situation where you should have said something, but you were afraid?

2.  How can your being willing to speak up be a blessing to someone else?

3.  Are you willing to be a mouth piece for God?

4.  Have you had someone to speak up for you? How did it feel?

# Prayer

*Lord, please help me to speak boldly for You. Bless the words of my mouth and the meditations of my heart. Please forgive me for the times that You wanted me to speak, but I kept silent. Use my mouth as Your mouth piece. Speak through me Lord!* **Amen.**

# *Do Right!*

*Choose to do the right thing!*

**Proverbs 31:9 (NKJV)**

*"Open your mouth, judge righteously,
And plead the cause of the poor and needy."*

*E*ach day we are faced with the opportunity to do right or to do wrong. As you get up, get dressed, leave your home and drive or walk to your destination, you are faced with decisions. You can either do right or you can do wrong. For example, when you get into a car and you are in a hurry, you can either go the speed limit or you can speed. When you come to a traffic light, you can stop or you can go through it. As you are going to work, you can be on time or you can be late. You can treat people kindly or you can be mean to others. You can choose to be a good wife/ mother and a good husband/father or a bad one. As a student, you can choose to be one who does the homework or one who does not. As a leader, you can choose to lead people astray or lead them the right way. Each of our choices affect us and other people so God wants us to do the right thing. Better than that, God wants us to do the righteous thing. He wants us to make the choice that lines up in accordance with His Word. We should make the choice that would bring glory and honor to God.

## *Embracing Excellence*

*Proverbs 31:9* says, "Open your mouth, judge righteously and plead the cause of the poor and needy." King Lemuel's mother was advising her son to do the righteous thing. She wanted him to not be afraid to open his mouth and to make righteous choices.

When our minds are weakened by wine, alcohol or sexual immorality and the things of this world, it affects our decision making. The king was responsible for making various decisions. The decisions that he made affected the lives of the people.

Many of us are in positions where we have to make decisions that affect others such as judges, lawyers, leaders, doctors, teachers, police officers, pastors or parents. It is so important that we speak with wisdom and make good decisions. The king's mom wanted her son to be the type of king who would take care of those who could not take care of themselves. She wanted her son to be concerned about the poor and the needy. She also wanted him to do his duties in such a way that justice would be given to all.

Perhaps God is calling us to do the same thing. Is there an area in your life where God wants to use you to speak, make a righteous choice or to make a decision that would help someone less fortunate than you? What is God calling you to do? Seek Him and obey!

## *Journal*

1. What does "doing right" mean to you?

2. Is there anything that you are doing and you know that it's not right?

3. Who does God want you to help?

4. Who is affected most by the decisions that you make from day to day?

# Prayer

*Lord, please help me to make righteous choices. Teach me to do Your will. Help me to realize that the choices that I make affect others.* **Amen.**

# The Ideal Wife

*Know what a woman of excellence looks like.*

**Proverbs 31:10 (NKJV)**

*"Who can find a virtuous wife?*
*For her worth is far above rubies."*

*I*magine that you are getting ready to purchase your dream home and money is not an issue. The builder has asked you to make a list of everything that you could possibly want in the house. Since money is not an issue, you begin to think of all of the luxuries that you have always wanted in a home. For example: A huge kitchen, a pool, a play room for the kids, a sun room, movie theater and an extra storage closet. The house will be perfect because it was designed with everything you could possibly want. This is your ideal house!

*Proverbs 31:10-31* is the beginning of a description of an ideal wife. The word ideal implies existing only in the imagination, conceived as constituting a standard of perfection or excellence, regarded as perfect of its kind. It is the portrait of what the ideal wife should look like. Some say that this is a standard for the type of wife that King Lemuel's mom would want for her son. Others believe that it is separate from her opening communication with her son. However, I think that it is interesting that verses 1-9 are a standard for a king given by his mother and verses 10-31 provide a standard for an ideal queen.

## *Embracing Excellence*

*Proverbs 31:10* says, "Who can find a virtuous wife? For her worth is far above rubies." I have heard many sermons about this scripture. However, when I first learned about the virtuous woman, I did not know that she was the ideal woman, and did not physically exist. I thought she was a person who existed like any other woman in the Bible. I later learned that the *Proverbs 31* Woman is a standard for all women. This woman is rare; she is a woman of excellence, moral worth and she is distinguished from the rest of the women. The qualities that she has are hard to find and priceless.

God has allowed this portrait of a woman to be in the Bible for a reason. What can we learn from her? God wants us to see the type of woman that He can develop in us. No one is perfect, but God is able to take the qualities of this ideal woman and shape and make us after His own heart. As we grow in our relationship with the Lord, He develops us and shapes us into the ideal woman. The Lord gives us a makeover as we make time for Him in our daily life. The closer we get to God, the more we become the ideal woman. You can't get closer to God without changing. When we embrace God and His Word, He changes our walk, talk, appearance and our behavior. We then become a woman of excellence.

## *Journal*

1. What are your thoughts about the ideal woman?

2. What does having noble character mean to you?

3. Why do you think this description of the ideal woman is in the Bible?

4. How do you want to be remembered?

## Prayer

*Thank You Lord for the portrait of this ideal woman. Please mold me and make me into the woman You want me to be. Help me to be a woman of excellence in my home, on my job, in my church and everywhere.* **Amen.**

# Can You Be Trusted?

*A person who can be trusted, is one who is treasured.*

**Proverbs 31:11 (NKJV)**

*"The heart of her husband safely trusts her;
So he will have no lack of gain."*

*M*y husband and I serve as facilitators for a class titled; "Building Your Marriage to Last." We love facilitating this class because we meet so many different couples who come together to hear God's principles concerning marriage. Some are newly married and some have been married for many years or married before. One of the husbands told me that the reason he was taking the class was to learn how to make a marriage work. He was eager to learn and to apply the principles because he had been married before and divorced. He said it was a marriage that didn't last long because he could not trust his wife. He was in the military, got married and had to go overseas to serve for a period of time. He said when he returned, his wife had spent everything he had and he had to start all over. He had been hurt and disappointed in how she had mismanaged the things that he left in her care. At the time, he did not have a relationship with Jesus Christ, so he had no hope and decided to divorce and start all over again. Now we know that there are two sides of the story, but the point here is that this man walked away from his marriage because he didn't feel like his wife could be trusted. Her actions and behavior left him in a bad place.

Many women want to be married but have not demonstrated that they can be trusted. Can you be trusted? To be trusted means that you can be relied upon. This also means a man can give you his cares, his valuables and not have to worry, because you will manage them well. Can he trust you to be responsible with the finances, children, the home and with managing his affairs? Are you the type of woman who can be relied upon? What kind of track record do you have? Can a man put his confidence in you and not be disappointed? Are you a woman of your word or do you typically say one thing and do another? If your husband were to give you money to pay bills, can you be trusted to take care of the bills or will you go shopping and spend the money on something else? Can he trust you to keep your body only unto him or will he have to worry about you sleeping with other men? If he gives you a house, can he trust you to make it a home? If the two of you make children together, can he trust you to raise a godly seed?

## *Embracing Excellence*

*Proverbs 31:11* says, "The heart of her husband safely trusts her; so he will have no lack of gain." God wants us to be women who can be trusted. A husband needs to be able to safely trust his wife. He should be able to rely on her to manage his affairs without worry or harm. As a trustworthy wife, a woman should be able to carefully manage everything assigned to her care. A husband should not have lack of or be robbed of anything because of his wife's poor management. A trustworthy wife should bring increase not decrease. A husband should be better as a result of his wife's management skills. The heart is the most vital organ; without it, there would be no life. A husband should be able to trust his wife with his heart.

## *Journal*

1.  Who was the first person that you learned to trust?

2.  Can you be trusted?

3.  Are you responsible with managing the affairs of your life?

4.  Do you normally keep your word? Why or why not?

# Prayer

*Lord, please help me to be a woman who can be trusted. Repair any areas in my life that cause me to not be a woman of my word. Teach me how to be a trustworthy woman.* **Amen.**

# *All the Days of Your Life*

*The way that you live now will determine what people say later.*

**Proverbs 31:12 (NKJV)**

*"She brings him good, not evil, all the days of her life."*

*D*eaconess Lynn Winters was a wife for 40 years and a mother of 3 sons. She loved the Lord and spent much of her time serving her husband, her family and her church. When her boys grew older, she would take time to pour into younger women. I became closer to her when she served in the Queen Esther Ministry as a facilitator. The Queen Esther Ministry is one that specializes in teaching women how to have a closer walk with the Lord. Deaconess Winters had a heart to serve and she loved working with women. The young ladies of the Queen Esther Ministry loved Deaconess Winters. She was the mom that some of the ladies did not have. While serving as a facilitator, Deaconess Winters was seriously ill and could no longer attend class. Unfortunately, she passed away before she could finish and before the ladies could graduate. I was later informed by her husband that she knew that she was sick when she made the commitment to serve. However, she wanted to be a blessing to the women for as long as she could. Deaconess Winters was a great facilitator and at the time, she had the largest class in Queen Esther. One of the things that was so amazing was that she did not lose one lady over the course of the 18 months that the ladies were in her class. Just as Deaconess Winters was known for doing good in Queen Esther, she was also known for doing good to her husband at home. She did her husband good all the days of her life. What a powerful legacy to leave. Have you ever thought about how you would like to be known? Wouldn't it be nice to be known for doing good all the days of your life?

# Embracing Excellence

*Proverbs 31:12* says, "She does him good, not evil, all the days of her life." This means that her husband did not have to worry about her causing him harm. Her actions and her behavior were good. What a way to be known. The way that you live your life right now, from day to day will determine how you will be known. If you want to be known for doing good and not evil all the days of your life, stay closely connected to God. It doesn't mean that you will be perfect. However, the goal of every Christian should be to please God all the days of our life. He is the only One who can help us leave a good legacy. Having a consistent relationship with God is the key to doing good consistently. For with God, all things are possible (*Matthew 19:26*). When we are committed to our relationship with God, He shapes us and molds us into the person that He wants us to become. This helps us to be an asset to any relationship. If we become a wife, we can bring our husband good and not evil because God is ordering our steps. When God orders our steps, we can be consistent with being a good woman, wife and mother.

# Journal

1.  How would you like to be known?

2. "All the days of your life." What are you doing now that does not represent the way that you would like to be known?

3. How can a relationship with God help you to be known for good?

4. How can you bring good and not harm to a person?

# Prayer

*Lord, please help me to live each day in a way that is pleasing to You. Show me how I can be used to bring others good and not evil. Help me to be obedient and to act on the things that will bring glory and honor to You.* **Amen.**

# Willing Hands

*Are you willing to do what God is calling you to do?*

**Proverbs 31:13 (NKJV)**

*"She seeks wool and flax,
And willingly works with eager hands."*

*O*ver the years, I have done several projects with my hands. I have created paintings, made baskets, lap scarves, ponchos, baby blankets, window treatments better known as curtains, I have upholstered chairs and altered clothing for friends. Each time that I have created something, I have been amazed at how well the projects have turned out. I can honestly say that each of the times, I wasn't sure how the projects would turn out, "but God." Once I got started, the Lord made a way for most of the projects to be a success. I say most, because I remember a painting that didn't turn out so well. Each project required faith because I knew what I wanted to make, but I wasn't sure if I could get my hands to create something that would be nice enough to display or to give as a gift. God would give me a vision of what the item should look like and I had to go to the store and select the right materials. Selecting the right materials, fabric and colors are very important.

One of the things that I find interesting about *Proverbs 31:13* is that the scripture says that she seeks wool and flax. Seek indicates that she had to go and find the materials. This shows her willingness. The materials were not brought to her. She had to put forth some effort. Back in the day, the Jews attached a woman's wisdom to her ability to use a distaff. It was important for a good woman to have sewing skills because she would make the clothes for her family and the needed items for her home. The wool was used to make the external garments and flax linen was used to make the inward garments. The men would only wear garments that were made at home by his wife, sister, daughter or granddaughter. So, this was a skill that was being taught to all of the women and girls in the family. The skill was being passed down so that the younger women could grow up and provide the same service to their husband. Today, very few women are sewing.

## Embracing Excellence

*Proverbs 31:13* says that "She seeks wool and flax and willingly works with eager hands." To willingly work with your hands is to work with pleasure and delight. The Lord wants us to willingly work with our hands. We should take pleasure and delight in using our hands to do whatever God has called us to do. A wife must be concerned about making sure that her husband is properly clothed from the inside out. Wool and flax are symbolic of the external and internal. What's interesting about the two materials is that they were not mixed. Only pure and natural fabrics were allowed to be used for the people of God. They were used for two distinct purposes. Wool was used for the external garments and flax linen was used for the internal.

Maybe you don't sew but you have a skill or talent that God has placed in your hands. God wants you to willingly use it to bless others. Whatever you have been given was meant to be used to bless your family, your church, your community and ultimately bring glory and honor to God.

## Journal

1. Do you have a willing attitude towards work? (In your home, on your job?)

2. What's in your hands? What kind of skills, talents or time do you have?

3. How can your skills, talents or time be used to bless others?

4. Who can you have to help you in using your skills to bless others?

# Prayer

*Lord, please help me to see the skills and talents that You have placed in my hands. Help me to work willingly. Give me a pleasant attitude so that I can bring glory and honor to You name.* **Amen.**

# What Are You Like?

*What word or words would someone use to describe you?*

**Proverbs 31:14 (NKJV)**

*"She is like the merchant ships,
She brings her food from afar."*

*O*n August 8, 2008, my husband and I celebrated our 10th Wedding Anniversary. We celebrated by joining another couple who was also celebrating their 10th Anniversary. Together, we went on a Royal Caribbean ship from Florida to the Bahamas. It was a trip to remember. This ship went from place to place transporting people with food, entertainment and everything that was needed to have a good time for a few days.

As I was studying *Proverbs 31:14,* I did a little research on ships and boats and learned that ships can be distinguished from boats based on their size, shape, cargo or passenger capacity. A ship is large and a boat is small but both are designed to work in the water. Merchant ships are used to transport passengers or cargo. Oftentimes they would have food, valuables or items needed for the home. Another name for it is a trading ship.

In Biblical times, excellent women were known for going far to secure the best food for their families. This is why *Proverbs 31:14* says the woman was like the merchant ship and that she brought food from afar. She had good trading and shopping skills and would go wherever she needed to bring food for her household. She knew how to trade something that she had of value in exchange for something that was on the merchant ships. She was known for trading in such a way that it benefited her family. The ships would bring in precious cargo that she couldn't get close by.

## Embracing Excellence

*Proverbs 31:14* says, "She is like the merchant ships, she brings her food from afar." This woman worked hard to be sure that her family was well supplied with the items and food that they needed. A merchant ship could have food, valuables or items needed for the home. What can we learn from this? God wants us to have skills and be willing to work hard to bring good things to our family. As women of God, we are to learn how to make the dollar stretch, go the distance if it means supplying our family with the best. We must be concerned about what we are bringing into our home. We must make wise purchases and allow God to use us to do things that are profitable for our households. Today, we are blessed to have the Internet which allows us to shop from afar and deliver to our door step. The *Proverbs 31* Woman made it her business to look for opportunities to buy items at the best price. She also knew how to make a trade. This is a valuable skill that I have been able to use. Many times we have skills and talents that we can exchange for something that we need and that someone else has. When a woman is resourceful and knows how to make the dollar stretch, she is a blessing to her family and her budget. Embracing excellence is about being skilled and resourceful.

# *Journal*

1.  What are you like? How would your family describe you?

2.  Do you know someone like the Proverbs 31 Woman (skilled, resourceful and willing to go the distance for you)?

3.  Are you willing to go the distance to bring in the best for your family?

4.  This woman is compared to a merchant ship; what would you be compared to and why?

# Prayer

*Lord, please teach me how to use the skills that You have given to me to bless my family. Give me wisdom to make profitable decisions. Help me to be willing to go the distance to bring good to my family and to others.* **Amen.**

# Rise Early!

*God has something special for all who are willing to seek Him early!*

**Proverbs 31:15 (NKJV)**

*"She also rises while it is yet night,
And provides food for her household,
And a portion for her maidservant."*

*I*t's been a few years since I wrote my first book. Each time that God gives me an assignment to write, I wonder how it will get done with everything else that I have on my plate. Every time that I pray about how I will be able to get something done, I hear God giving me the same answer, "RISE EARLY!" When I was wondering how I would have time to write this book, God said, If you are willing to rise early, I will speak to you and give you the words to write. He told me to trust Him for every word. God held true to His word. Each morning I would begin by praying and reading scripture. Oftentimes, the verse did not make sense to me but after seeking God, and reading the verse several times, I was able to get a word. The Holy Spirit would give me understanding and insight on each verse.

Throughout scripture, there are so many places where God met people early in the morning. One of my favorite verses is "O God, You are my God, early will I seek You; My soul thirsts for You; My flesh longs for You in a dry and thirsty land where there is no water" (*Psalm 63:1*). I have found that rising early helps me to hear God more clearly than any other time of the day. Also, I am able to get more done because I have fewer distractions. Rising early for me is around 4:00 a.m. As I committed to rising early, God was faithful at meeting me every morning with a word. Rising early to seek God blesses God and therefore, He blesses us.

## Embracing Excellence

*Proverbs 31:15* says, "She also rises while it is yet night, and provides food for her household, and a portion for her maidservants." The *Proverbs 31* Woman rises early to provide whatever her household needs and to get her house work done. She is concerned about her family and her maidens. From this, we can learn to rise early and to think about the needs of our family and others. Rising early helped her to be prepared for the day. The scripture says that she would rise early to provide food for her family. In addition to her gathering natural food, I also see this as gathering spiritual food. When I rise early, I pray and seek God for the day ahead of me. God speaks and feeds me spiritually so that I am able to have something to give to my husband, children and all who come into my presence. It is often in the early morning that He places other people on my heart to pray for or to connect with them.

Are you willing to rise early to seek God? God will never disappoint you. There are special treasures in store for those who rise early! Embracing excellence requires making God your first priority and seeking Him early.

## Journal

1. Are you an early riser or a late night owl?

2. Are you willing to rise early to seek God?

3. How can rising early bless God?

4. What is the key to you being able to rise early?

# Prayer

*Lord, help me to rise early! Give me all that I need to prepare for the day and to give my family what it needs for today. Lord, please help me to rise early to provide for my family and those You would have me to bless.* **Amen.**

# Purchase and Profit

*Many know how to shop and spend money but few know how to make a profit.*

**Proverbs 31:16 (NKJV)**

*"She considers a field and buys it; From her profit, she plants a vineyard."*

*I*f I had to pick an area of my life that I have made the most mistakes, I would say in my finances. Especially before marriage. I wish that I had been taught early on how to save, spend, invest and make wise financial decisions. Finance was not taught at school. As a result, many of the things that I have learned, I had to learn the hard way. Here are a few things that I wish that I had learned earlier in life.

1. Think carefully before you spend your money.

2. Whenever you make money, tithe, save and then spend.

3. Don't spend everything. Always save something for a rainy day.

4. Consult with others who are wise with the dollar.

5. Create a budget and learn to use it.

6. When making a big decision, consult with people who have already made that decision.

7. Find out lessons learned and learn from them before you make a purchase.

8. Do your homework, compare prices, and think carefully before you purchase. Check online.

9. Ask yourself; "Do I really need this? Is this a good purchase?"

10. Live below your means and not above.

When you make wise financial decisions, you will be able to make a profit so that you can have money to do other things.

God wants us to be good stewards over the money that He gives to us. He also wants us to have so that we can be a blessing to other people.

## Embracing Excellence

*Proverbs 31:16* says, "She considers a field and buys it from her profit, she plants a vineyard." She carefully considered a field before she purchased it. When you carefully consider something, you think about it, give attention to it, examine it and then make a decision. It's so easy to see something and immediately purchase it (especially when you have the money) without spending any time considering whether or not it's a wise choice. We must learn to wait and pray before we spend. One of the tricks of the enemy is to get us to make fast and wrong decisions. We must be wise with our purchases. Considering the field first would allow this woman to make a choice that would bring a profit and she was able to plant a vineyard. This means she was able to plant a vineyard and increase her produce. She had an increase because she knew how to wisely make a purchase.

## Journal

1. Do you make good financial decisions?

2. Do you have a budget?

3. What are two financial lessons that you have learned and can share with someone else?

4. Why is it important to think carefully before making purchases?

# Prayer

*Lord, please forgive me for all of the times that I did not take the time to think or pray before spending money. Help me to do Your will with the money that You give me. Make me a good steward over everything that You place in my hands. Allow me to make decisions that will be profitable.* **Amen.**

# Spiritual, Physical and Mental Fitness

*God wants you to be in good health;
spiritually, physically and mentally.*

**Proverbs 31:17 (NKJV)**

*"She girds herself with strength,
And strengthens her arms."*

*O*ne of the things that I have been trying to consistently incorporate in my life for almost 30 years is exercise. I have not mastered it. Every week, I press to get 3-4 days of exercise. For the most part, I accomplish this goal, but all it takes is one thing to get me off track, and I can easily skip working out. I have always been concerned about my weight because my grandmother said the women in our family are prone to be heavy and that we have "big bones." I later learned that being big boned is not a medical term. However, it is a term used to refer to the fact that people have different sized frames. People with larger frames have a tendency to be bigger according to the American Academy of Orthopedic Surgeons. However, the size of your frame is not the reason for being overweight. They say a larger frame may be the reason for a couple of pounds but not an extra 30 or 40.

Since I believed that I was prone to be heavy, I have worked very hard at trying to maintain my weight. Over the years, my weight has gone up and down. Maintaining has really been a challenge because I love to eat. When I was in my 20's and 30's, I would exercise here and there. I would walk and at one point, I joined a gym. After turning 40, I noticed a change in my body like never before. I realized that I could not eat the same way or the same things without moving my body. Eating a lot with little or no movement equals gaining weight. I decided that if I was going to maintain my weight, I had to do a combination of watching what I eat, controlling my portion size and exercise. Once I started being consistent 3-4 times a week, I noticed a difference in the way that I feel. Exercise gives me energy, helps me to maintain my weight and good health. The benefits are so great that I can't afford not to move my body.

In addition to exercise, we must be spiritually and mentally fit. Maintaining spiritual fitness requires praying, reading and applying God's Word on a daily basis. Going to church and participating in spiritual activities also helps. Having a daily diet of God's Word helps to maintain spiritual and mental fitness. I have found that reading good books is another discipline that helps with maintaining spiritual and mental fitness. I also like to read for personal growth. Mental fitness includes eating healthy, exercising, getting the proper sleep and rest. For as little as 10 minutes a day, you can read something that will increase your knowledge and teach you something new. Strive to learn something new every day; it helps to sharpen your mental fitness.

## *Embracing Excellence*

*Proverbs 31:17* says, "She girds herself with strength, and strengthens her arms." This verse lets us know that she knew what gave her strength and she used it to strengthen herself spiritually, mentally and physically. When you are spiritually, mentally and physically fit, you have the energy to get the job done. Whatever the task with business, school, ministry or any assignment that you have been given, you will do it better when you incorporate spiritual, mental and physical fitness in your life. When you feel good spiritually, mentally and physically, you are in a better position to help someone else. It's hard to help someone when you are beat down, tired and exhausted.

# *Journal*

1. Do you exercise? Why or why not?

2. What are the benefits of exercise?

3. What makes you feel spiritually and mentally fit?

4. Are you typically energetic or out of energy?

# Prayer

*Lord, please help me to maintain being spiritually, mentally and physically fit. You know where I am weak. Help me to improve in that area. Give me accountability so that I can be committed. Remind me of Your truth in III John 1:2 that says; "Beloved, I wish above all things that You may prosper and be in health, even as Your soul prospers." Equip me with everything that I need to be better for You and to live better.* **Amen.**

# Good Merchandise

*Know your worth!*

**Proverbs 31:18 (NKJV)**

*"She perceives that her merchandise is good,
And her lamp does not go out by night."*

When I was in junior high school, I took a sewing class and learned how to sew. I was so excited because my mom was a seamstress, and I had watched her make outfits. Although I made clothing while I was in the sewing class, outside of class, I really didn't practice using my sewing skills until I became an adult. Once I got married, had children and became a stay at home mom, I decided to pick up my sewing skills and start making some items for profit. I put a lot of time and effort into picking out the fabric, colors and sewing things just right. I made a variety of items such as satin pillow cases, hair bonnets, ponchos, lap scarves and baby blankets. I knew that if others were going to be interested in buying anything, my merchandise had to be good. If I was working on a sewing project for someone, I would stay up late to get the job done. One of the challenges that I often encountered was determining how much to charge for something that I made. I knew my merchandise was good, but I had difficulty determining what it was worth. I learned that it is so important to know the worth of your merchandise. Otherwise, you will spend more time working and not get properly compensated for your materials, time and skill. Just as I needed to know the worth of my merchandise, you need to know your worth. You are valuable to God and whatever He has given you to do has value.

# Embracing Excellence

*Proverbs 31:18* says, "She perceives that her merchandise is good, and her lamp does not go out by night." In other words, she senses the worth of her work and is not in any hurry to call it quits (NKJV). The word perceives means that she became aware of or she came to the knowledge of the fact that her merchandise is good. She made sure that it was good and profitable. She did whatever it took to complete the task. Sometimes we don't realize that we are good and that God created us to do good. I love the fact that the *Proverbs 31* Woman was wise enough to have an income-producing business with good merchandise, and she was able to be a blessing to her house hold. We must know that God has called each of us to work with Him and for Him. Whatever God has called you to do is good and you must be confident. He has a plan and a purpose for each of us and wants to use us in different places. Be encouraged to use the skills, gifts and talents that God has given you to do work that will bring glory and honor to God. God is able to use your skills to produce merchandise that is good and profitable.

# Journal

1. What do you enjoy doing?

2. What services might you provide for profit?

3. When working on a job, are you willing to put in extra time to make sure that the job gets done?

4. What are your skills, talents, or hobbies?

# Prayer

*Lord, thank You for the skills and talents that You have given me. Help me to use them to bless others and to produce a profit that will bless my family. Help me to do whatever it takes to complete the tasks and to finish what I start.* **Amen.**

# Use Your Tools

*I have tools, you have tools, all of God's children have tools.*

**Proverbs 31:19 (NKJV)**

*"She stretches out her hands to the distaff, And her hand holds the spindle."*

*I* started working during my junior and senior year of high school. My first job was in the government working as a clerk typist. I was a part of a program called COE which is the abbreviation for Cooperative Office Experience. I went to school for a half day and worked the other half of the day. I loved it! I was able to go to school, go to work and gain skills in a business office. It was great! What was really nice was when I began to get a pay check with my name on it. I had a great teacher who helped me to get into the government. One job led to another job, and I was gaining lots of experience. Little did I know that the skills and training that I was getting would help to provide me with a good foundation. I gained on-the-job skills and experience that helped me to have the right tools for my future.

## Embracing Excellence

In *Proverbs 31:19,* the woman is found stretching her hands to the distaff. A distaff is an instrument used for spinning wool or flax. She also holds a spindle, a slender rounded rod with tapered ends used in hand spinning to twist and wind thread from a mass of wool or flax held on a distaff. This woman had to have skills to know how to use the distaff and the spindle. She had one in one hand and one in the other. She was working with these tools to make garments. She was using tools to help her get the job done. Not only was she working and using her tools, she did this right before her maidens. She was setting an example of work right before her maiden's eyes. She provoked them to work by working herself. She knew how to use her tools to get the job done. She didn't think it was beneath her to do a job that her maidens could do.

Although this profession may not be popular today, women are still working and using tools. What kind of work does God want you to do? Are you already doing it or is it something that you haven't started?

## *Journal*

1. How can you use the tools that you have to bless someone?

2. Does the work require you to use tools? (computer, phone, etc.)

3. What class, training or preparation can you take or make to build your skills?

4. What skills do you have and what skills would you like to develop?

# Prayer

*Lord, I thank You for all of the work that women do all over the world. Show me what You want me to do. Help me to do what You have called me to do. Reveal the necessary tools that I need to use. Help me to be an example that will bring glory and honor to You.* **Amen.**

# Concerned About Others

*It's not all about you!*

**Proverbs 31:20 (NKJV)**

*"She extends her hand to the poor,
Yes, she reaches out her hands to the needy."*

*A*bout 6 years ago, my husband and I decided that I would do something that I had never dreamed of doing, homeschool our children. My daughter was going to the 6th grade and my son was going to the 3rd grade and they both asked me to homeschool them. They had been exposed to homeschooling through our church and had met other families who homeschooled. One evening we all went to dinner and after dinner, they popped the question. I immediately looked at my husband and his response was, "try it, if it doesn't work, they can always go back to a regular school." So I left teaching at a private school and came home to homeschool both my son and my daughter. I had taught in a public school for 7 years, then a private school for 3 years and at that time, we all believed that God was calling me to homeschool. I do believe that it is a calling. God was calling me to pour into my own children. One of the benefits of homeschooling is that students take the required courses along with anything else that you decide you want to teach. As their teacher, I would select curriculum to teach the standard information for their grade level, and I would decide what else I wanted to add to enrich their educational experience.

One of the things that I wanted my children to learn is to be concerned about others. Take time out of your schedule to help others. Not only did I want them to help out at our church or with the people that we knew, I wanted them to also be concerned about people who are outside of our church. As a result, I searched for an opportunity and experience that would allow my kids to do something for others.

We connected with the Central Union Mission in Washington, D.C. and served on a regular basis. Each month, we would help serve at their Senior's Luncheon. My kids and I would serve lunch to the senior citizens, assist in playing games and help to provide a church service for the senior citizens. We were so happy and excited about serving them. The seniors often expressed how happy they were to see the young people helping to serve. I believe that this experience taught my children to be willing to serve others and to be concerned about others. As a result, last year they both decided to serve on their first mission's trip. At the age of 12 and 14, they became missionaries and served with a Mission's team in Detroit. Their mission was to help the less fortunate in fixing up their homes on the inside and the outside. I was so blessed by the fact that they wanted to serve as missionaries and show their concern for others.

## *Embracing Excellence*

*Proverbs 31:20* says, "She extends her hand to the poor, yes, she reaches out her hands to the needy." This woman was concerned about the poor and the needy and she made herself available. No matter what you have or don't have, there is always someone who is less fortunate than you. Whether you realize it or not, you are rich and you have so much to offer someone who is poor. God wants to use you, your hands, time, skills and if necessary, your finances to bless those who are less fortunate. We all have something to offer. God wants us to be concerned about others so that they can feel His love. God works through people to bless others. When you show your concern for the less fortunate, you demonstrate the love of Jesus. This is so important because we can be used to win others to Christ. It is with love and kindness that people are drawn to Christ (*Jeremiah 31:3*).

# *Journal*

1. Are you willing to help the poor and the needy?

2. What can you do to help the poor and the needy?

3. Are you normally concerned about others or are you self-centered?

4. Why do you think God wants us to be concerned for others?

# Prayer

*Lord, please help me to be more concerned about others. Show me ways that You would have me to help the poor and the needy. Help me to realize that people can be poor and needy in body, mind or spirit.* **Amen.**

# *No Fear!*

*God has not given us a spirit of fear!*
—II Timothy 1:7 (NKJV)

**Proverbs 31:21 (NKJV)**

*"She is not afraid of snow for her household,
For all her household is clothed with scarlet."*

*L*et it snow, let it snow, let it snow! In the winter of 2014, the D.C., Maryland and Virginia area experienced quite a bit of snow. Children were out of school for so many snow days that some schools were not able to make up all the days. For many, the school year had to be extended until the last week of June. Each time that a snow storm was predicted, there were a few things that I noticed. 1) The grocery stores would be crowded. 2) Some of the stores ran out of things like milk, bread and toilet paper. 3) The shelves were getting empty and the stores had not been able to keep the shelves stocked. Oftentimes, people become afraid when a snow storm is predicted because there are so many uncertainties.

The goal that everyone seems to have is to make sure that their household has everything that it needs. Stores that sold salt, shovels and things that are used to clear the snow usually get bombarded with large crowds. Some even go to department stores to make sure that their family has warm clothes, boots, hats and heavy coats. Parents want to make sure that their children have everything that they need to keep warm in the cold weather. Parents who are good planners usually purchase their kid's boots, coats, hats, scarves and warm clothes before the winter comes because they know it is coming. When you are well prepared, there is no fear.

## Embracing Excellence

*Proverbs 31:21* says, "She is not afraid of snow for her household, for all her household is clothed with scarlet." This woman is not afraid of the snow; she has no fear because she has provided everything needed for her household. One of the greatest lessons that we can learn from this is that she is prepared. No matter what type of storm you are facing, God can help you to prepare. Preparation is often a good remedy for fear. In my experience, the more preparation, the less fear.

The *Proverbs 31* Woman has provided for the needs of her family and takes comfort in knowing that her household will be protected with warm clothing. All of her household is clothed with scarlet. Scarlet is usually a red color and in some cases it can be purple. The color is deep, warm and used to retain heat. She had no need to fear, because she had prepared her household for the snow. Now maybe you live in an area where it doesn't snow; if this is the case, you probably have to prepare for hot days, rain or earthquakes. Each type of weather requires some preparation. The main point is, no matter what you are facing, there is no need to fear. God will be with you, and He will help you. Preparation is the key!

## *Journal*

1. What do you do to prepare for a storm?

2. Identify the things that cause you to fear.

3. How do you handle your fears?

4. Has being prepared ever helped to decrease or eliminate your fears?

# Prayer

*God, I know that fear does not come from You. Help me not to worry or fear. Teach me how to trust You for every need. Lord, please provide all that I need so that I can make sure that my family has everything it needs.* **Amen.**

# Well-Decorated and Well-Dressed

*Decorate and dress in a way that is attractive.*

**Proverbs 31:22 (NKJV)**

*"She makes tapestry for herself;
Her clothing is fine linen and purple."*

*T*wo of my favorite things to do are to decorate and to dress. I love picking out colors, furniture, pictures, comforters and curtains. Although decorating can be very costly, there are so many ways to make a room feel nice and cozy without spending a lot of money. You can start with something as simple as paint and pillows. If the color of the room makes you feel good, you can start with that. It is so important to create a space that is inviting to you and your family. Your home should be your private sanctuary. The home is the foundation for all who are raised there. Home is where our stories begin. It should create an atmosphere of love, peace and joy. Home should also be a place of order. It's a training ground for so many things such as; cooking, cleaning, respecting others, maintaining order, sharing, learning how to treat others, learning responsibility, etc. The way that a home is decorated can set the tone, mood and the atmosphere for you, your husband, children and everyone who enters. What do people see, feel or experience when they enter your home? Does your home show that you have spent some time and thought on each room or do you treat your home like a truck stop? You don't plan to be there for long and don't spend much time in it, so you haven't taken the time to decorate. Decorating your home can make everyone feel warm and comfortable enough to spend time there. Without decorations, a house may not feel like a home.

The other thing that I love to do is to dress. I love to get dressed up and I love putting together outfits from day to day. It's something about deciding what colors to wear, and coordinating colors that I love. I love creating an outfit and finding accessories to match. Looking good from the inside out brings glory and honor to God. We must always remember that we represent Christ wherever we go. Here is how you start getting dressed from the inside out. You start by getting dressed with prayer and spending time in God's Word. This helps to get your mind, soul and spirit together. After you have had time to dress your insides, then you can decide what to wear on the outside. It is so important for women of God to present themselves in a way that is pleasing to God and to their husbands if they are married. Before people learn anything about you, they see how you present yourself.

## Embracing Excellence

*Proverbs 31:22* says, "She makes tapestry for herself; her clothing is fine linen and purple." The *Proverbs 31* Woman made coverings, cushions and decorations for herself. Her home was well-decorated with the things that she made. She created an environment that she, her husband and family wanted to come to. In addition, her clothing is fine linen and purple. She was well-dressed and covered. She took time to pick out the best fabric for her clothing and was well put together. Her physical house and her body were well dressed. A man loves to come home to an attractive home and an attractive wife.

## Journal

1. How do you feel about the way that your home looks?

2. Do you need to do some decorating to your home?

3. How do you feel about the way that you present yourself? If you are married, ask your husband if he is pleased.

4. Do you dress well from the inside out? How can dressing well and decorating well bring glory and honor to God?

# Prayer

*God, thank You for the place that You have given me to call home. No matter what the size of my home is, help me to create an inviting environment. Please help me to decorate my home well and to dress well. Bless my home to be a warm and attractive place where people can feel Your love and warmth.* **Amen.**

# A Good Reputation

*Every day, you are creating a reputation for yourself.*

**Proverbs 31:23 (NKJV)**

*"Her husband is known in the gates,
When he sits among the elders of the land."*

*I*t has been said that, "Behind every great man, there's a great woman." That great woman is normally his wife and if he's not married, it could be his mother. If you look at the men who have excelled in their education, careers or in ministry there is often a great woman who inspired them. I love seeing men give honor to their wives and their mothers because these women have supported and encouraged them to be the best that they can be. Somehow, many of these women learned how to work, raise their children, and take care of their domestic affairs in such a way that has encouraged these men to rise to the top. Look at our President, Barack Obama and many of our famous basketball players and entertainers who have excelled in their careers because of the influence of a woman.

When you find a great man and hear his background, you will hear the story of how his wife is such a great supporter or how his mother raised him well. A woman can help to make a great man or she can break him. A woman with a good reputation can help to make a great man.

## *Embracing Excellence*

*Proverbs 31:23* says, "Her husband is known in the gates, when he sits among the elders of the land." Part of the reason that her husband is known in the gates is because of his wife's reputation. She represents him so well that she makes him shine in the gates. God designed the woman to be a helper. The best helpers have a close relationship with God. When a woman is closely connected to God she will have a positive impact on her husband or anyone in her presence. A woman can help a man to become all that God wants him to be.

The *Proverbs 31* Woman has a good reputation. Everyone knows how good a woman she is. Her reputation makes people want to know the man that she is connected to. A man is proud to have a wife with a good reputation; it speaks volumes to everyone who sees it. He can sit confidently, because she has built a reputation around practicing the Word of God. Her relationship with God creates a good reputation.

# *Journal*

1.  What words would you use to describe your reputation?

2.  What does it mean to have a good reputation?

3.  What makes a bad reputation?

4.  Do you think that God is pleased with your reputation?

# Prayer

*God, please help me to live my life in such a way that I have a good reputation. Forgive me for the things that I have done that may have had a negative impact on my reputation. Help my reputation to be a blessing to everyone who comes around me.* **Amen.**

# Working Woman

*Whether you work in the home or outside of the home, you are a working woman.*

**Proverbs 31:24 (NKJV)**

*"She makes linen garments and sells them, And supplies sashes for the merchants."*

*I* started working my first job when I was in the 11th grade. My job title was Clerk Typist and I worked in the government. My first job led to my second job, then to my third and fourth job. Each of them were in the government. I worked in the government off and on until I graduated from college. Whenever I came home for the summer or Christmas breaks, I had a job working. I have always enjoyed working and making my own money. After I graduated from college, I went from working in the government to working in private industry. I worked for one company for about three years and then decided that what I really wanted to do was teach. I left the private company and got a job teaching high school. I absolutely love teaching! So from 11th grade on, I have always worked, enjoyed working and enjoyed making my own money.

In 1998, I got married and one year later we had a baby girl. Two years after the first child, I had a baby boy. When my first child was about two years old and my second was about to be born, my husband and I made a decision for me to leave my job as a school teacher and to come home full-time. This was a big decision because at this point, I had been working outside of the home most of my life. This decision required a lot of prayer, faith and sacrifice, but we felt it was the best move for our family. God challenged us to live on "Faith Boulevard" and to trust Him like never before. We accepted the challenge. The purpose was so that I could focus on raising a godly seed and be the primary caretaker for the gifts that God had given to us. It bothered me that I was spending most of my time pouring into hundreds of other people's children and had very little time and energy to spend with my own children. So I came home to be a stay-at-home mom and worked very hard in the home. I refuse to say

power, love and a sound mind." Whenever the enemy tries to get us to embrace fear, (False Evidence Appearing Real) we must cling to God's truth.

## *Embracing Excellence*

*Proverbs 31:25* says, "Strength and honor are her clothing; she shall rejoice in time to come." The *Proverbs 31* Woman is strong and secure. She can rejoice about the future because she knows that she and her family are covered by God. She wears strength and honor as her clothing because she is looking forward to a fabulous future. Fabulous means exceptionally good, unusual, marvelous and incredible. This is the kind of future that God wants us to have. This woman has done everything possible to prepare for her future. She has labored, made profits for her family and has peace of mind. Therefore, she is confident and cheerful about her future.

## *Journal*

1.  How do you feel about your future?

2.  What are you doing now to prepare for your future?

3. What are three things that you see happening in your future?

4. Do you know your temperament?

# Prayer

*Lord, help me to do all that I can do now to prepare for my future. Help me to make proper preparations for my family and me. Give me Your peace about my future and whatever You have in store. Bless my future to be fabulous!* **Amen.**

# A Wise Tongue

*Be careful about what you say and how you say it!*

**Proverbs 31:26 (NKJV)**

*"She opens her mouth with wisdom,*
*And on her tongue is the law of kindness."*

*O*ne of the things that has increased over the years since I've been a Christian is the time that I spend reading and studying the Word of God. The time that I spend in God's Word refuels me, strengthens me, provides direction, wisdom, insight and the list goes on and on. There are so many benefits to studying God's Word; however, the one that I love the most is getting wisdom. Wisdom is knowledge that can only come from God. It is knowing what is true or right. Wisdom is when God gives you discernment and insight that can only come from Him. The wonderful thing about wisdom is that all we have to do is ask God for wisdom and He gives it freely. *James 1:5* says, "If any of us lack wisdom, let him ask of God who gives to all generously and without reproach, and it will be given to him."

When we get wisdom from God, it changes the way that we live, think, how we treat others and how we speak. When a woman spends time in God's Word, studying and applying what the scripture says, she will become wise. Her conversation will be different because when she speaks, wisdom will come out. Words are powerful and it is so important that we examine what we are saying. Are we saying words that will build up or tear down? Are we speaking kindly or are we speaking in an angry or nasty way? Does wisdom come from our tongue or does foolishness? As a teacher, one of my goals is to always put information in so that I will always have something to give out. The more that I read and study God's Word, the more wisdom He gives me to share. As I spend time with God, He gives me wise counsel and instruction for my life as well as for me to share with others. God wants to use us in the lives of our families, friends and others, but we have to take in God's wisdom so that we can have it to give out.

# Embracing Excellence

*Proverbs 31:26* says, "She opens her mouth with wisdom, and on her tongue is the law of kindness." The *Proverbs 31* Woman opened her mouth with wisdom. Since wisdom comes from God, she had to be spending time with God to get wisdom. When God gives us wisdom, it's not just for us to keep it to ourselves; it's for us to share it with others. Someone else can benefit from the wisdom that God gives to you. The other benefit of wisdom is that it changes your tongue. As women of God, it is important that we speak with kindness. The Bible says that it is with loving-kindness that He has drawn us and we must do the same to draw others to Christ (*Jeremiah 31:3*). There are enough mean people in the world. The law of kindness will be on your tongue when you spend time in the Word of God. Kindness is one of the fruits of the spirit and it often comes out of a relationship with God. (*Galatians 5:22-23*). The fruit of the Holy Spirit is the result of the Holy Spirit's presence in the life of a Christian. When the Holy Spirit is present, we can speak with the law of kindness. God wants us to be wise and kind, but we must have a relationship with Him. Having a relationship with God means that we have accepted Him as Lord and that we spend time with Him so that we can imitate Him.

# Journal

1. Do you speak with a wise tongue?

2. Would your friends, co-workers and family say that you speak with wisdom?

3. How can you get more wisdom?

4. Do you speak with kindness on your tongue?

# Prayer

*God, please help me to be mindful of the words that I speak. Bless the words of my mouth and the meditations of my heart to be acceptable in Your sight. Teach me to put wisdom in so that wisdom comes out.* **Amen.**

# Keeper of the Home

*If you are going to be a keeper of your home, you must spend time in it.*

**Proverbs 31:27 (NKJV)**

*"She watches over the ways of her household,
And does not eat the bread of idleness."*

*L*ife can be so busy! When there is work, school, activities and events to attend, we can find ourselves spending less time at home. Do you ever have days where you miss your house or where you just long to spend time at home and not have to go anywhere? I have days like that and usually when I feel this way, I have been on the go with events and activities that have required me to be away from home. It's nice to have things to do and places to go, but if you don't have some form of balance, you can spend so much time out of the home and not enough time in the home. Now if you are single, you may have a little more freedom in this area. However, if you have children or are married, you have to be intentional about spending time at home. Home is where your story begins. It should be your very own ministry center. Each room has a purpose and things that need to be done. If you don't spend much time in the home, your household will suffer in some way, unless you have people taking care of everything for you. A marriage will suffer when attention is not given to it. Children will suffer if there is no one in the home watching over them. Spending time in the home allows one to be present and to see what's going on. Parents need to be aware of what's coming in and going out of their home. A good keeper of the home needs to be fully aware of what's going on in the home.

I can never say that I don't have anything to do at home. There is always something to do as I watch over the affairs in my home. There is cooking, cleaning, organizing, laundry, etc. Watching over the home means being attentive to the needs of the home. A home needs to be well stocked with food and supplies that are used throughout the home. When you are in tune with these things, you know when you need toilet paper, soap, etc. In *Titus 2:4,* Paul encourages women to be keepers of their home and reminds us that it is very important to be present.

## Embracing Excellence

*Proverbs 31:27* says, "She watches over the ways of her household, and does not eat the bread of idleness." In the first part of this verse, we see that the *Proverbs 31* Woman is attentive to her household. It is very difficult to be attentive if you are rarely home. It's easier for the enemy to come into our homes by way of drugs, bad music, bad company, disorder and sex outside of marriage if we are rarely home. The second part of the verse says that she doesn't eat the bread of idleness. This means that she does not sit around eating just to be eating. She is not eating the bread of idleness because she has things to do. It is important to be active and not idle. Eating and idleness can lead to gaining weight. Before we eat, we should ask ourselves, "Am I really hungry?" If not, we should not eat. We must keep it moving. The *Proverbs 31* Woman is handling her business at home and therefore, there is no time for idleness.

## Journal

1. Are you pleased with the amount of time that you spend at home?

2. Is there anything or any room of your home that needs more time or attention?

3. What does it mean to be idle?

4. What's the problem with idleness?

# Prayer

*God, thank You for my home. Please help me to be a good keeper of my home. Make me alert and aware of everything pertaining to my home. Teach me Your will and Your way for my household. Help me not to eat the bread of idleness, but to be busy doing what You would like for me to do.* **Amen.**

# *Eyewitnesses*

*Be careful about how you live from day to day, somebody is always watching you.*

**Proverbs 31:28 (NKJV)**

*"Her children rise up and call her blessed;*
*Her husband also, and he praises her*
*Her husband also, and he praises her."*

*H*ave you ever watched the news and listened to the story of an eyewitness? An eyewitness is a person who sees some act, occurrence or thing and gives a firsthand account of whatever took place. Eyewitnesses are those who know you best. As a mom and a wife, my primary eyewitnesses are my children and my husband. They are around me every day, watching my daily actions. They see the way that I live, they see the way that I keep the house, give instructions, how I treat people, how I talk to people, how I handle business from day to day and how I live out my Christianity. If anyone can attest to my walk with God, it would be my children and my husband. I am truly blessed because of the children and husband that God has given me. Oftentimes, when I feel like I am at the end of my rope, God uses one of them to encourage, inspire or challenge me. One of the reasons that I have been able to serve in ministry for over 10 years is because I have been encouraged, supported and strengthened by my family.

We must always remember that we are being watched by those who are closest to us and sometimes there are others watching from afar. The eyewitnesses who live in your home have a full view of you. They see you when you are up, down, happy, sad, energetic or tired. They watch the decisions that you make from day to day. We must be careful about the way that we live our lives before our eyewitnesses.

## *Embracing Excellence*

*Proverbs 31:28* says, "Her children rise up and call her blessed; her husband also, and he praises her." Her children and her husband are able to call her blessed (happy and fortunate) because they have been watching her. The *Proverbs 31* Woman lives her life in such a way that her children and husband show her honor and respect. They had firsthand knowledge of her care, her love, the way that she lives and conducts herself from day to day. Her husband is so blessed by the way that she lives until he gives her praises.

## *Journal*

1. Who are your eyewitnesses?

2. What do you think they see when they see you?

3. Is there anything that you don't want your eyewitnesses to see?

# Prayer

*God, I thank You for my eyewitnesses. Help me to live my life in such a way that my eyewitnesses are blessed. Help me to watch the way that I talk and walk. Teach me how to be a good example for my eyewitnesses to see. Shape me, mold me and make me.* **Amen.**

# Excels Them All!

*A woman of excellence will stand out!*

**Proverbs 31:29 (NKJV)**

*"Many daughters have done well,
But you excel them all."*

*W*e live in a world where we hear lots of negative words about husbands, wives and marriages. Have you ever heard a husband praise his wife? It may be rare, but whenever I hear it, it is like music to my ears. When a man expresses his approval or admiration for his wife, it's a wonderful thing. By praise, I mean that a husband speaks well of his wife and is grateful for her being a good wife, mother (if she is one) and for her commitment to God. He gives God praise for the wife that God has given him.

My husband is really good about giving me praise. He often says, "I know God loves me by the wife that He gave me." He is not a writer, but one day I was evaluating myself to see how I am doing in this category so I asked the question, "How do you feel about having me as your wife?" Here is his response:

> *I feel blessed to have a wife like you and I believe I'm a better man because of you. I appreciate the love and obedience you have for God. The Word says, he who finds a wife, finds a good thing. I found the best thing. I feel it most when we minister to couples, how two people from two different backgrounds have a passion for the same thing. If I was with someone else, I probably would not know that this part of my life was even there so I am so thankful for that.*

I was so blessed by his words that I wanted to share them with you. Notice that within the word praise is the word raise. When a husband praises his wife, it helps to affirm her and lets her know that she is appreciated and vice versa. Everyone needs to know when they are doing a good job. Words of praise are encouraging. These words should not be given to boost one's ego, but it's like giving them flowers while they can smell them. When my husband speaks well of me, it makes me want to do more. I am energized to give more of myself to him and my children.

## Embracing Excellence

*Proverbs 31:29* says, "Many daughters have done well but you excel them all." This woman is blessed because both her children and her husband are speaking well of her. In this verse, her husband is blessing her. Obviously, he is aware of the precious gift that he has in his wife. He realizes that there are many women out there who have done well but his wife surpasses them all. She is an outstanding woman! Women who love God and have a close relationship with Him should stand out from the crowd. The Bible says, if you love Him, you will obey Him (*John 14:15*). Obeying God brings excellence in the way that we talk and walk. The more we obey God, the more we walk in a spirit of excellence. Embracing excellence will cause a woman to excel them all!

## Journal

1. How do you feel when someone gives you a compliment?

2. If you are married, how would your husband describe you? What do you think he would say about you?

3. If you are not married, how would a close friend describe you?

4. What does excelling them all mean to you?

# Prayer

*God, please help me to be like the virtuous woman and to excel them all. Teach me to live my life in such a way that everyone around me can speak well of me. Help me to notice when people are outstanding and to use my words to encourage them. Bless me to excel in all that I do.* **Amen.**

# Fear God

*Real fear should lead to obedience.*

**Proverbs 31:30 (NKJV)**

*"Charm is deceitful and beauty is passing,*
*But a woman who fears the Lord, she shall be praised."*

*I*t's a pleasure to see a woman who is beautiful from the inside out. A woman who has charm and beauty has a great combination. Charm is defined as attractiveness and beauty is the quality that gives pleasure or deep satisfaction of the mind. There are many women who are applauded for their attractiveness and their beauty, but the Bible says that these things will pass. Have you ever seen a picture of a woman in her younger years? Her skin was youthful, her hair was full and her body was beautifully shaped. Sometimes the picture doesn't look anything like the person today. As the years go by, and a woman ages, her charm and beauty will fade but the quality that will remain is her fear of the Lord. Fearing God doesn't mean being afraid of God, it simply means having reverence and so much respect for God that you want to choose to live right. Living right is about obeying the Word of God.

There is something special about women who are beautiful on the inside and the outside. What's even more precious is an older woman who loves the Lord. No matter what her age or how her physical qualities have changed, she is beautiful because of her relationship with God. I believe that obedience to God makes us radiant and keeps us looking good in our older years.

## Embracing Excellence

*Proverbs 31:30* says, "Charm is deceitful and beauty is passing, but a woman who fears the Lord, she shall be praised." This verse makes it clear that charm and beauty will fade away. As much as

I desire to be beautiful from the inside out, I realize that the most important thing is my relationship with God. You can have all of the latest and the greatest when it comes to looking beautiful, but if you don't have a relationship with God you are missing it. Things are temporary but a relationship with God is eternal. God longs to have an intimate relationship with each one of us. When a woman fears God, she will be admired and praised.

## Journal

1. What does fearing God mean to you?

2. Do you fear God?

3. What are the benefits of fearing God?

4. List two women whom you admire. What is it that you admire most?

# Prayer

*God, please help me to reverence You in such a way that others can see. Give me a hunger and a thirst for You so that my behavior lines up with Your will. Make me beautiful from the inside out.* **Amen.**

# *There Are Rewards*

*God rewards those who diligently seek Him.*
—Hebrews 11:6 (NKJV)

**Proverbs 31:31 (NKJV)**

*"Give her of the fruit of her hands,
And let her own works praise her in the gates."*

*H*ave you ever been to an awards ceremony? As a little girl, I can remember being in school and at the end of the school year I would get awards for different things that I accomplished during the school year. Some of the awards were for perfect attendance, honor roll and good behavior. Whenever I was honored for any of these things, I would also get rewarded by my parents. They would take me out to eat or purchase something that I really wanted or give me a special gift. Whenever I was rewarded, I felt good, my parents were happy and it encouraged me to keep doing well in school. I never wanted to do anything or have behavior that would cause my parents shame. Only good! Therefore, I worked hard to make good grades, stay on the honor roll and was a good student throughout my years of being educated. Just as a good student is rewarded with good grades and accolades, a great woman or wife should also be rewarded and honored.

God favors great and godly women. He loves when women are obedient to His Word and godly. When godly women are married, their husbands are truly blessed. A man who has an excellent wife wants to praise her. Not only praise her, but honor and reward her. Rewards and honors should motivate and encourage us to keep doing what God wants us to do. When a man or a woman, boy or a girl fear God and work very hard to be their best, they will be rewarded and honored. I am a witness that God is a rewarder to those who diligently seek Him.

# Embracing Excellence

*Proverbs 31:31* says, "Give her of the fruit of her hands, and let her own works praise her in the gates." This woman was rewarded and honored by her husband. He acknowledged all of the work that she had done. He was attentive to the work that she was doing. Giving her the fruit of her hands is giving her rewards for the labor that she has done. She was exceptional and her works brought her praise. When we see a woman who is excelling as a wife, mother or woman of God, we should take the time to recognize the fruit of her hands. Not every woman is to be rewarded and honored. Some women do not deserve honors and awards because of laziness and foolishness. However, the *Proverbs 31* Woman was exceptional and godly; therefore, she was praised by her family.

What type of woman are you? Are you living a life that should be praised? Are you godly and excelling in your role as a wife, mother, business woman or godly woman? The *Proverbs 31* Woman made great accomplishments in her home business, finances, etc. She used her abilities to bless her husband and her children. With God's help, you can do the same. You were created to be a blessing to others. As you spend time with God He will develop and place excellent qualities in you. A woman of excellence will be rewarded by God!

# Journal

1. How are you doing in the roles that you play? (in your home, on the job, in the church)

2. Have you ever been rewarded for a job well done?

3. How does it feel to be rewarded?

4. What lesson can you learn from the *Proverbs 31* Woman?

# Prayer

*God, I thank You for the example of the* Proverbs 31 *Woman. Thank You for everything that I am because of my relationship with You. Teach me to live a life worth rewarding and honoring. Help me to embrace excellence.* **Amen.**

# About The Author

*Carolyn Tatem* is an author, speaker, teacher and a licensed minister. She is the author of *Marriage from A to Z* and *Marriage from A to Z for Singles*. For several years, Carolyn has served as the Director of The Queen Esther Ministry, a ministry that specializes in training and discipling women at First Baptist Church of Glenarden in Maryland. Many have been changed through her ministry. She and her husband, William serve as leaders in the Couples Ministry. They have been married for 17 years and have 3 children.

For more information and speaking engagements, please contact the author at:

www.carolyntatem.com

*Connect on Twitter:* @carolyntatem

# Acknowledgements

I thank God for giving me this assignment and giving me the words to write each day. I thank my husband and children for all of their support and help on this project. I especially want to thank all of the women in my life who have helped me to embrace excellence.

# Other Books by
# Carolyn Tatem

*Marriage from A to Z*
   (Principles for a Successful Marriage)

*Marriage from A to Z Study Guide*
   (Workbook for Married Couples)

*Marriage from A to Z for Singles*
   (Study Guide for Singles and those preparing for Marriage)

*Blog:* www.marriagefromatoz.org

# References

Matthew Henry's Concise Commentary.

LaHaye, Tim. The Spirit Controlled Temperament. Tyndale House Publishers, Inc, 1994.

Life Application Study Bible. Tyndale House Publishers, Inc. 2005.

CPSIA information can be obtained at www.ICGtesting.com
Printed in the USA
LVOW10s1454071215

465787LV00020B/1123/P